Core Math Skills
Measurement and Geometry

I Can Draw Shapes

Shapes and Their Attributes

Luke Wojick

PowerKiDS press™

NEW YORK

Published in 2014 by The Rosen Publishing Group, Inc.
29 East 21st Street, New York, NY 10010

Book Design: Mickey Harmon

Photo Credits: Cover, pp. 5, 22 Mircea Netval/Shutterstock.com; pp. 7, 9, 11, 13, 15, 17 (hand) Lipskiy/Shutterstock.com;
pp. 7, 9, 11, 13, 15, 17 (sketchbook) nuttaki/Shutterstock.com; p. 19 iStockphoto/Thinkstock.com; p. 21 (table)
donatas1205/Shutterstock.com.

Wojick, Luke.
I can draw shapes: shapes and their attributes / by Luke Wojick.
  p. cm. — (Core math skills: measurements and geometry)
Includes index.
ISBN 978-1-4777-2055-4 (pbk.)
ISBN 978-1-4777-2056-1 (6-pack)
ISBN 978-1-4777-2231-2 (library binding)
1. Geometry—Juvenile literature. I. Title.
QA445.5 W65 2014
516—dc23

Manufactured in the United States of America

CPSIA Compliance Information: Batch #CS13RC: For further information contact Rosen Publishing, New York, New York at 1-800-237-9932.

Word Count: 163

Contents

Learning to Draw

Drawing shapes is fun!
I can make many things
from different shapes.

5

I can draw a triangle.

I draw 3 lines.

I draw 3 corners, too.

I draw a rectangle with 4 sides.

2 sides are short.

2 sides are long.

What's a Trapezoid?

I draw a triangle and a rectangle together.

This makes a shape called a **trapezoid**.

Drawing Squares

A square has 4 sides.

I make each side the same size.

Each corner is the same size, too.

Half Circles

I like to draw half circles.

A half circle has 1 round side and 1 flat side.

I draw 2 half circles.

I can put them together to make a circle.

17

I cut out a half circle.

I bend the half circle down the middle.

I bring the flat edges together so they touch.

This makes a **cone**!

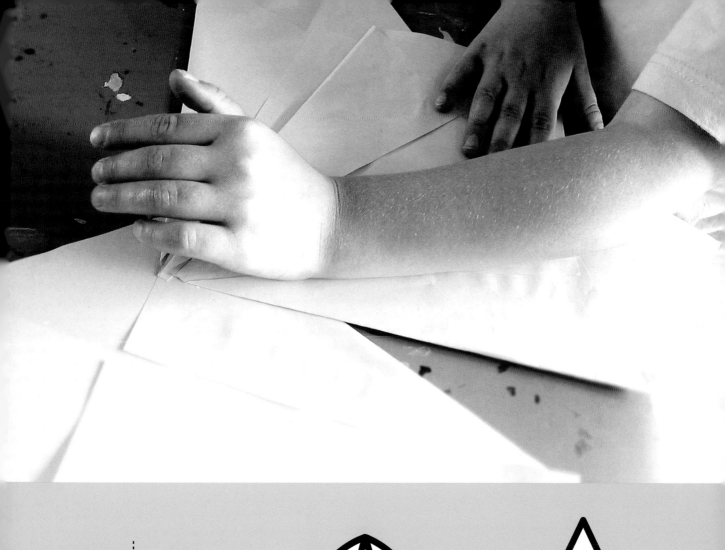

I make a paper cone in art class.
Then, I take it home and show it
to my mom.

21

What Can You Draw?

It's fun to make shapes!

What can you make with shapes?

Glossary

cone (KOHN) A solid shape that is round at one end and pointed at the other.

trapezoid (TRA-puh-zoid) A shape with four sides that can be made by putting a rectangle and triangle together.

Index

Due to the changing nature of Internet links, The Rosen Publishing Group, Inc., has developed an online list of websites related to the subject of this book. This site is updated regularly. Please use this link to access the list: **www.powerkidslinks.com/cms/mg/icd**